HISTORIC BOSTON

AMERICAN LANDMARKS

Jason Cooper

The Rourke Corporation, Inc.
Vero Beach, Florida 32964

PHOTO CREDITS:
© Frank Balthis: page 7; © Susan Cole Kelly: title page, pages 4, 10, 12, 13, 15; © James P. Rowan: cover, pages 8, 17, 18; © Lynn M. Stone: page 21

CREATIVE SERVICES:
East Coast Studios, Merritt Island, Florida

EDITORIAL SERVICES:
Susan Albury

Library of Congress Cataloging-in-Publication Data

Cooper, Jason, 1942-
    Historic Boston / by Jason Cooper
        p. cm. — (American landmarks)
    Includes index.
    Summary: Describes some of the historic places where Boston's patriots lived, worked, battled, and argued against British rule including the Massachusetts State House, Faneuil Hall, and the Old North Church.
    ISBN 0-86593-546-7
    1. Historic sites—Massachusetts—Boston Juvenile literature. 2. Boston (Mass.)—Buildings, structures, etc. Juvenile literature. 3. Boston (Mass.)—History Juvenile literature. [1. Boston (Mass.)—Buildings, structures, etc. 2. Boston (Mass.)—History. 3. Historic sites—Massachusetts—Boston.] I. Title. II. Series: Cooper, Jason, 1942- American landmarks.
F73.37.C66 1999
974.4'61—dc21   99-27477
                                                              CIP

Printed in the USA

TABLE OF CONTENTS

HISTORIC BOSTON

Boston, Massachusetts, is famous for its Celtics, Red Sox, and baked beans. It's also famous for its role in American history, especially the early days. Faneuil Hall in Boston is known as the United States' "Cradle of Liberty."

In the 1760s, Boston was the largest city in the Massachusetts Bay Colony. Like the other 12 **colonies** (KAH luh neez) in America, Massachusetts was controlled by Great Britain.

This is the Bunker Hill Monument in Boston.

Great Britain had started the American colonies in the early 1600s. But by the 1760s, most of the **colonists** (KAH luh nists) had been born in America. Many of them wanted freedom from British rule and British taxes. They were called **patriots** (PAY tree utz), and Boston had more than its share. Among them were Paul Revere, Samuel Adams, John Hancock, and James Otis.

In 1775, American **militiamen** (muh LIH shuh min) and British soldiers fought battles at Lexington and Concord, near Boston. Those battles began the Revolutionary War, America's fight for freedom from Great Britain.

Minuteman National Historical Park covers 1,000 acres in three towns near Boston. Here an artist paints a monument in Concord.

In the years leading up to the revolution, Boston's patriots helped shape American **opinion** (uh PIN yun) against the British. The events of those years made not only Boston's history, they made American history.

Many of the **historic** (hih STOR ik) places where Boston's patriots lived, worked, battled, and loudly argued against British rule have been **preserved** (pruh ZERVD). One such place is the Old South Meeting House. Five thousand angry patriots gathered there in 1773 to protest a tea tax.

Dorchester Heights Monument in Thomas Park, South Boston, honors the actions of General George Washington in March 1776.

THE STATE HOUSES

The present Massachusetts State House was built in 1798. The land beneath and around the state house was once grazed by John Hancock's cattle. The state house is the oldest building on Beacon Hill.

The Old State House, built in 1713, is a different building. It stands today as the oldest public building in the city.

Patriots listened as someone read the Declaration of Independence from the Old State House balcony on July 18, 1776. Afterward, they ripped symbols of British rule from the roof and burned them.

The Old State House, built in 1713, stands on the site of Boston's Towne House, built in 1657 and destroyed by fire in 1711.

The steeple of the Old North Church signaled to Paul Revere. Revere rode to awake the "Minutemen"—citizen soldiers who could be ready to fight the British "in a minute."

The U.S.S. Constitution, *"Old Ironsides," rests at the Charlestown Navy Yard in Boston. The Bunker Hill Monument rises in the background.*

FANEUIL HALL

Faneuil Hall was the site of many loud, fiery meetings in old Boston. The building was built in 1742 by Peter Faneuil. He gave the building to Boston as a gift.

When the British began a tea tax, patriots gathered here to protest. They decided at Faneuil Hall that they would fight against British "taxation without representation." In other words, the patriots felt that it was unfair to be taxed by Great Britain unless America had a vote in British affairs.

Patriots and protesters against British rule often gathered at Faneuil Hall. The first floor was once a market. Damaged by fire in 1761, Faneuil Hall reopened in 1763.

THE CHURCHES

The Old North Church, built in 1773, is the oldest church in Boston. This church will always be linked to the famous ride of Paul Revere on April 18, 1775.

Patriots arranged to use the steeple of the church to send lantern signals. The number of burning lanterns would tell Revere how the British soldiers were moving—by land or by sea. Revere and patriot William Dawes saw the signal. Then they rode into the countryside to wake the militiamen. It would be the job of these farmers, tradesmen, and ordinary men to load their guns to fight the British.

King's Chapel was designed by America's first architect, Peter Harrison. Harrison's plans called for a steeple which was never built. The church was completed—without the steeple—in 1754.

Paul Revere's house, built around 1680, is preserved in downtown Boston. Revere lived there from 1770 to 1800.

King's Chapel was built in 1754. In its burial ground next door are several famous Americans. Among them is Mary Chilton, the first woman to step off the *Mayflower* in 1620 at Plymouth Colony. Also buried here are William Dawes and John Winthrop. Winthrop was the first governor of Massachusetts Bay Colony.

The Paul Revere House, built around 1680, is the oldest building in downtown Boston. It's one of 16 stops along the Freedom Trail of historical sites.

OTHER SITES

The list of historic sites in greater Boston is lengthy. At the Charlestown Navy Yard, the U.S.S. *Constitution* is still afloat. She was launched in 1797 and fought the War of 1812 against the British. She became known as "Old Ironsides," because the oak planks she was built from were strong enough to deflect cannon shots. One sailor said, "Her sides must be made of iron."

A stone monument 221 feet (67 meters) tall marks Bunker Hill. Patriots faced British soldiers here in June, 1775.

Near Boston, Minuteman National Historical Park in Concord is the site of the first Revolutionary War battles.

This site marks the grave of British soldiers in Minuteman National Historic Park, Concord.

GRAVE OF BRITISH SOLDIERS
"THEY CAME THREE THOUSAND MILES, AND DIED,
TO 'KEEP THE PAST UPON ITS THRONE:
UNHEARD, BEYOND THE OCEAN TIDE,
THEIR ENGLISH MOTHER MADE HER MOAN."
APRIL 19, 1775.

VISITING HISTORIC BOSTON

One of the best ways to enjoy historic Boston is a walking tour of the Freedom Trail. Ninety-minute tours with a guide begin at the National Park Service Center. They are available April through September.

The tour takes visitors to 16 historic places along the Freedom Trail route.

The Freedom Trail Foundation, a not-for-profit group, helps preserve sites along the trail.

Visiting the Freedom Trail is a great way to learn more about the beginning of America.

GLOSSARY

colonist (KAH luh nist) — one who helps settle a new colony or who lives in a colony

colony (KAH luh nee) — a place settled by people who keep ties to their former nation; a place apart from but ruled by the nation that started it

historic (hih STOR ik) — famous or important in history

militiamen (muh LIH shuh min) — citizen soldiers who are available to fight in emergencies

opinion (uh PIN yun) — a view or judgment formed in the mind about a particular matter

patriot (PAY tree ut) — one who loves his or her country and supports its causes

preserve (pruh ZERV) — to keep safe from danger or destruction

INDEX

FURTHER READING

Find out more about historic Boston with these helpful books and information sites:

- Cater, Alden R. *The American Revolution.* Franklin Watts, 1992.
- Kent Deborah. *Lexington and Concord.* Children's Press, 1997.
- Penner, Lucille R. *The Liberty Tree: The Beginning of the American Revolution.* Random House, 1998.
- The National Park Service on line at www.nps.gov